PANCHROMATIC OBSCURITY

Richard Foley

BALBOA.
PRESS

A DIVISION OF HAY HOUSE

Balboa Press books may be ordered through booksellers or by contacting:

Balboa Press
A Division of Hay House
1663 Liberty Drive
Bloomington, IN 47403
www.balboapress.com
1-(877) 407-4847

Because of the dynamic nature of the Internet, any web addresses or links contained in this book may have changed since publication and may no longer be valid. The views expressed in this work are solely those of the author and do not necessarily reflect the views of the publisher, and the publisher hereby disclaims any responsibility for them.

The author of this book does not dispense medical advice or prescribe the use of any technique as a form of treatment for physical, emotional, or medical problems without the advice of a physician, either directly or indirectly. The intent of the author is only to offer information of a general nature to help you in your quest for emotional and spiritual well-being. In the event you use any of the information in this book for yourself, which is your constitutional right, the author and the publisher assume no responsibility for your actions.

Any people depicted in stock imagery provided by Thinkstock are models, and such images are being used for illustrative purposes only. Certain stock imagery © Thinkstock.

Printed in the United States of America.

ISBN: 978-1-4525-8149-1 (sc)
ISBN: 978-1-4525-8150-7 (e)

Balboa Press rev. date: 10/15/2013

NOTE OF EXPLANATION

Poetry is merely imaginations inditing and reiterating
various subliminal scenarios.
Anything is possible deep within the realm of the mind.
Create and vanquish.

THE DISTORTED SOUL,
RICHARD LAYTON FOLEY

AMBIVALENT ECLIPSE

Polemics are the powerful magnets that reign to my
left and my right,
I'm the metal that's being pulled on both sides
simultaneously,
Split directly down the center I hear my ego echo,
Inexorable pride is the only thing that remains inside,
Sun shines so bright while moon provokes the night,
Derived from the infest nest,
Perfidy peevishly pierces,
Probity promotes prodigies,
Desire hotter than fire,
Ridiculous race destroyed by the insidious pace,
Rather be stuck in a wave than a cave,
Birds and bats fly,
Can we be trusted that high?
Does the condescending shatter?
Will the mending matter?
Brains or chains?
Life or strife?
Pay the steep price,
Delay the cheap vice,
Seductive reputation rebukes,
Splendid duplicate approves,
Terrified of the excruciating pain,
That drives me so insane,
Afraid of the known instead of the unknown,

Too familiar this disappointment is prone,
Predicament that stings inside of the heart,
Wishing that none of this ever had to start,
She thrills the exhilarating flirt,
Dread the bitter dessert,
Have you ever abhorred and cherished somebody so
much that your relationship is Siamese twins?
Leering into the tawdry reflection,
Ostentatious mirror exaggerates the aristocracy…

CYNICAL ACCURACY

Born in a coffin,
Buried in my mother's womb,
Give me a jacket it's getting cold in here,
Give me a straitjacket it's getting crazy in here,
I'm begging somebody to not disappoint me,
I dare someone to show me some probity,
Where are you?
Do you exist?
Are you out there somewhere lurking?
Or am I merely muttering to my thanatological self?
Prurient repertoire is pouring down the fabulous
funnel,
Cordoning her vulnerable alliance that cries in the
tomographic tunnel,
Alleviation only vilipends dawdlers,
Who are you?
Do you really know?
Do you even care?
Endorsing a fleece into the muzzle,
Forcing a piece into the puzzle,
Ensnare the naked widow,
Stare out the wicked window,
Too sturdy to fall,
Too dirty to call,
Brutal box is insidiously withering the world down
deeply into this obsession of irony,

Deliberate delay always comes into play,
Contagious contaminations continue contriving,
Sacred semantics shocking somberly,
Nefarious lemur attacks with nociceptive dominion,
I can only feel the collusion,
Does it really have the ability to effectively persuade?
Repeat the brilliant abandonment,
Rescue their fancy debate…

HUMANITY VANITY
CALAMITY INSANITY

Scared to read the next page,
Don't want to get stung by the abstruse rage,
Attempting to descry the bountiful sage,
So I can be released from this squalid cage,
Impossible to open the pertinacious door,
Dependable room must protect the venerable floor,
Transcendent key you cannot ignore,
Unlocked what you see you adore,
My mind stays spinning,
Eavesdrop on the dinning,
We are riding into the twenty seventh inning,
Irrelevant who is winning,
Appears vastly distant yet on the brink,
Inevitable for this ship to sink,
Chaos and disaster pretend not to link,
Desperately refusing to think,
Precocious chance,
Splendid trance,
Devastating prance,
Relentless dance,
Disloyal crown,
Royal clown,
Turmoil town,
Spoil frown,

Skeptical sun burns the inexorable blizzard,
Miserable moon chills the querulous lizard,
Crystal ball resents the procrastinating wizard,
They constantly hinder everyone with their shrewd
vizard,
Better bluff with the jack of spades,
The queen of hearts invades,
Exposed the reticent escapades,
Ethereal fiasco reluctantly fades,
Collecting her vindictive file of punitive dreams,
All of them prevail by abusing the virtuous screams,
Lucrative fluke detects her impeccable teams,
Irascible insect precludes what this seems,
Why do you let?
Why do you fret?
Why do you regret?
Why do you forget?
Answers slay the questions as the leaf owns the tree,
Solutions dilute the problems as the key immune to
being free,
Sometimes you got to be blind to sincerely see,
There's you and here's me…

FROZEN BEACH

While I explore I descry the cold shore and icy ocean,
Kids build snowmen instead of sandcastles,
Adults skate instead of surf,
Ebbed to a polar halt the glacial tidal wave had a dark
green tiger shark bulging out of it,
Icicles dangle from this pelagic predator's exquisitely
sharp teeth,
Crevices and fissures are established beneath my feet,
Frigidly sinking into the sea ice cube I finally realize
the immaculate truth,
Incapable and/or unwilling to share this I wonder,
Why now?
Why this particular method?
I guess it is all a part of the plan,
Even though they are all wearing swimsuits,
I'm still gathering around the notion that,
I am the sole soul who is wandering in a coat...

ESSENTIAL PROPAGANDA

Clay drips off their fabrication that poses as a
concerned face,
Refractory sludge accumulates inside of their ears to
the extent of primary hindrance,
Why do they ask us questions when they cannot hear
our answers?
Controversy lingers through their despotic climax,
Perpetually they dote their own relentless power trip,
Trying to steal their ravishing helm would be merely
futile,
Anticipation for the expiration of the stale imbroglio
disappeared when they extracted the hazardous
strings,
Penguin chases the snake,
Genuine traces the fake,
Atrocious aspects assuring,
Ferocious concepts enduring,
Sir ice burns,
Her entice discerns,
Sometimes it's fun,
Sometimes it's well done,
Sometimes the moon despises the sun,
Fatigued due to the wanton journey only to discover
that we are totally incapable of being exculpated from
this never ending nightmare,

Hope ignites the frilly fuse,
Chain reaction of ordeals burns closer toward the stick
of discreet dynamite,
Life explodes into the taboo time,
Time is a cryptic crime,
Gigantic lofty dudgeon drives the corrupted car on the
bedizened highway,
Wry wreck is inevitable,
Bitterness you learn to savor,
Sweetness you return the favor,
Climb the tenacious fountain,
Swim in the permcable mountain…

SEDATE FATE

Inflict conflict,
Reprobate concentrate,
Complete defeat,
Scratch attach,
Contribute attribute,
Stereotype gripe,
Learn burn,
Aware unfair,
Adore core,
Savage ravage,
Realize demise,
Ignite light,
Strange derange,
Confess depress,
Top drop,
Keen queen,
Wince prince,
Wreck check,
Browse arouse,
Incest quest…

MALICE IN WONDERLAND

Mad hater never seems to enjoy the precious game,
Harmless violence stretches across the benevolent
forest,
Only to contaminate the purest,
Shiny imagination and dim compass is all you need
for survival,
Judges rap their guilty gavels,
Hedonistic jester contemplates on the acrid dupery,
Elite epiphanics transpire from the purple poisonous
giraffe,
Cloying venom trickles down into the wizard's cups,
What were they drinking anyway?
Hunting for their secrets is futile,
They won't let you in,
Wasting your time trying to comprehend them insults
their existence,
Understanding is too demanding,
Awake inside of a dream,
Asleep inside of a reality…

RIPE TYPE

Cloning incubators is *their* tourniquet,
Rise above *their* cold masks,
Saponaceous towers lurk in front of *their* bathtub,
Jump inside of *their* suspicious ideas,
Rejection reflection stoically ruins *their* immaculate
moment,
Wolves fly under *their* clairvoyance,
Curious fish mounted on *their* dry dam,
Frozen procedures melt *their* hot contradictions,
Winter's rivalry summer steals *their* limpid seasons,
Vivid volcanoes write with *their* lava ink pens,
Arrayed scars haunt *their* impossible vestige,
Wires stretched out of *their* fungus,
Discipline wreaks *their* preposterous guidance,
Peculiar reputation circulates *their* liberty,
Parlous jargon taunts *their* silent negotiation,
Seductive throne abandons *their* dire duplicate,
Appalling horse uninvited by *their* pensive exile,
Precise error damages *their* perfervid translation,
Their their their their their their their...

METAL GALAXY IN MY POCKET

Silver rain leaks from the esoteric cloud,
Blood shines all over their discreet souls,
Magnificent moon ran into a desolate policy,
Reticent storm whistled sneeringly at the belligerent
intuition,
Incorrigible map guides validly,
Liquid castles stand firm and sturdy,
Anaerobic stars lick irrational drama,
Ironic window eats dusty views,
Reluctant existence burns beneath and above the
fugacious sky,
Preening her laminated isolation irretrievably,
Vindictive encore vaguely sacrifices the prominent
and scanty retribution,
Wooden lake drips uninvited scorpions,
Promises dwell in the cold snow…

THE LIZARD OF AWES

We're off to steal the lizard,
The chaotic lizard of awes,
Because, because, because, because of all the crazy
things he does,
Tornado randomly spun her and her little dog too,
Assumptions established that the house landed
aimlessly,
Follow, follow, follow, follow the blue brick road,
Witch of the East was the ultimate target,
Beautiful magical slippers is conveniently Dorothy's
size,
Lions and tigers and bears oh lie,
Conniving and beguiling and conspiring oh my,
Pay no attention to the charming reptile behind the
curtain,
Scarecrow seeks for a stray shadow,
Tin man looks for a migratory zeitgeist,
Lion searches for a baneful legend,
Dorothy rummages for a rancorous utopia,
There's no place like tome, there's no place like tome,
there's no place like tome…

PETROUS RAIN

Pouring down demolishing the humanoid duplicates,
Shouting for some kind of purity,
Detecting these empty plants,
Comforting this delicate dirt,
Plummeting into gentle roofs,
Harming odd mammals rapidly,
Ruling every possible threat,
Clawing a treasonable voyage,
Jeering at the gullible grass,
Wondering how to nullify the thick robust creek...

EPIC POLTERGEIST

Death crawled in my bed on one portentous occasion,
I chased her away with a sharp imagination,
Maybe she won't wake up in the morning,
Maybe all our ordeals will disappear in the middle of
the night,
Sun bites the moon,
Run fights the swoon,
She is the thief and I am the gold,
Uncertainty looms,
Frisky dawn released the psychoanalytic yawn,
Elaborate dream haunts me in the evening's ploy,
Choleric ghost jeopardizes this loutish tenet,
Touching plenty of sensitive spots,
She should be exiled,
Strangled by the vacuum cleaner's cord,
Accidentally forsaking the ignited candles,
Dracula lurking through the smoke discerning,
Kills fish,
Spray can project,
Remember the day in the woods?!
Bassett girls are wack,
Does drugs make you do that?!
Only the animals can hear the music…

RABID ROUTE

Are you positively sure you want to go this way?!
What if it leads to destruction?!
What if it bleeds dysfunction?!
What if there is no other alternative?!
Where will you end up?!
Where still you send erupt?!
Where the contentment dies?!
How can you just sit there?!
How than you must not care?!
How is this universe squelching?!
When does the lock open the key?!
When can the dock close the sea?!
When you say with the appeasable anchor?!
Who do you admire?!
Who do you desire?!
Who is smiling in the corner?!
Stars drown?!
Planets suffocate?!
Magical fraud convinces the circus?!
Grizzly bears cooking ice cream on an Indian wagon?!
I seem to be trapped inside of an esoteric spiral?!
I dream of camphoraceous chimneys contemplating
about abducting fire?!

ALEATORY ALIBI

Searching diligently for the essential key I discovered
that it is irrelevant to being authentically free,
Rummaging for something that does not exist while
trying desperately to create it,
Love is the ingravescent pain that resides inside of my
immedicable heart,
Tergiversate around a verisimilar dream,
Exonerated because you parry the constant mulish
pursuit for distraught,
Dusty windows envy clear mirrors,
Risky experiments morph into loyal addictions,
Tragic habits chased magic rabbits out of the
incantational hats,
Slander is the toxic crime,
Maybe you were at the lazaretto during the
calumniation,
Claiming that you were at two places at once,
Perhaps the sky swallowed the sun and the moon
simultaneously,
Innocent by chance,
If animosity could kill then everybody would be dead,
Abide genocide…

IMPOSTERS GALORE

Why don't you just forsake your sentimental mask?
Roaming around in your ersatz atmosphere,
Vindictive composure lingers in your pathetic world,
I despise your disguise!
Still unconsciously gazing at yourself?
You thought you were looking at me,
In reality all you see is the chagrined image in the
mirror,
I defeat your deceit!
When are you going to jump out of your fraudulent
shell?
Depending on your camouflaged campaign is on the
Endangered Species List,
Sever that atrocious anchor that weighs everybody
down,
I destroy your decoy!

STAGNANT WELTSCHMERZ

I'll never be free! Not truly free anyway. Even if I get out of this depraved horrible place that does not deserve to exist I still won't be free! Wherever I wander I'll never break these invincible chains that weigh me down so perpetually! It's not places that I so desperately and futilely try to escape. It's not people that I so resentfully and grudgingly attempt to flee from. Oh no it's much deeper than that! Its emotions haunt me more than anything!

Feeling agonizing torture for some sort of... How can I forsake these sentimental obstacles?! What if I could change everything that I wanted to change?! Then would I have really changed anything?! Would it change unfortunate pain that burns in my esoteric core?! Trade yesterday for tomorrow? Why?! When you know for certain what happened yesterday but you have no clue what will occur tomorrow. Even if yesterday's regretful events are so dreadful that you would be willing to trade them for any of tomorrow's unknown results could quite possibly somehow be far worse than anything yesterday can disgustingly offer! Who?! Who can unlock these dirty filthy fetters?! I've searched, rummaged, foraged, and sought for pure impeccable freedom! I even tried to settle for just a tiny piece of liberty! Perhaps I should... Despite my earnest efforts to understand any of this I am stoically aloof simultaneously! How can I win this bizarre game?! This game that constantly changes its rules without any permission from anybody?! This game without a name.

This game that has no mercy on anybody who relentlessly refuses to roll the vice dice?!

How?! Tell me if you immaculately know! Tell me even if you slightly know! Flying in a fabricated sky posing as a limitless nirvana I remember that I'm still and will always be confined to this cage… This cage that laughs at me every single day. This cage that smirks at the very notion of me being released. This cage that monitors its own structure to make sure it's too concretely strong for me to fledge out and defeat this isolation! Fade into the distant illusion… Plenty of things have been said but nothing makes any sense! If we say different words they will finally comprehend. If we say it in a more esoteric or intelligent way they will surely comprehend! No not this time! Imagine being in a box that opens and closes consistently. Interesting and dull things come and go. Yet you can't do anything but just curl up in an irrelevant corner and observe. Experience teaches you not to get attached to anything that passes through this assembly line of… Everything that enters also exits regardless of how much you approve or disapprove. Lingering inside of this grotesque box is your primary purpose no it's your only purpose… No! Scream for help! Whisper to the walls of this arrant box! Neither shall free me! Basking with women is my paramount craving! Programmed to seduce and trick. After establishing trust and loyalty I am embarrassed and humiliated! How could I possibly allow them to blind me so vulnerably?! How indeed?! Stench of hypocrisy abrades this entire box that focuses on Operation Misery… Mission includes no choices or decisions. Fret not for they do not think for themselves!

Fact of the matter is they can't think for themselves! They won't let us... It won't let us... Surrounded by the high walls of this internal chaos... wings are thwarted out before they can even be contrived! Swimming through them requires enough imagination to ignite a flame hotter than the very fire that burns beneath my integrity! Few people actually carry such a remarkable and noble characteristic! Trust me I know! I've made it my life long pursuit to find such contributes! Most people don't even possess the slightest... Naturally unfaithful they connive their way through everything manipulating machines of... Deny defy pry sigh try why cry lie die... Plagued by their own betrayal! How can you guide a blind vision?! Mirrors shattered shards flattered! Jesters and clowns play with the blade of grass... Stare if you dare I don't care you don't compare to this lair of unfair unjust nightmare... Its walls melt with my hope of liberty! Maybe that fire will combust this box lost out of the shambles... game in this box fools even the rules... Sculpt up around this slithering reflection that withers and blossoms simultaneously! Help! Help... Help me help you help them help us for we finally by some miraculous lucky maneuver have escaped this transgression! Fresh air swoops in and we disobediently breathe! Inhale and exhale this glory! Inhale and exhale this spruced up fantasy! Indeed that is what it is! Box of propaganda laughs in the distance! Or wait it sounds like... yes... it's not far away at all... its close... so close its mockery touches

the very core of our polished and spruced up reputation!
Feel the walls of the box diminishing into tiny particles
of… Neglect care! Ignore care! Delete care! Care is an
unnecessary barrier… walls… but not the walls of the box
oh no not their walls… not their box…

We are locked upside down! We are locked up inside out!
We are locked indefinitely! Wait a minute! Wait a second!
Wait for however long you want or need! We can imagine
ourselves through this heinous box of negative energy!
They invented this box before everything existed including
themselves! They are everyone in your life that has been
jealous! Everyone who has not wanted to see you prosper
and succeed because they know that they can't! Everyone
who has never believed in anything you ever did or
endeavored to do! Everyone who has never believed in you!
Everyone who has never believed in themselves! Everyone
who has never believed in anything! Anything at all!

So they invented a false world that conquers everybody
else before they even get started! The box! Our natural
proclivity for negative energy!

Negative energy lives in this box where its walls are
surrounded…

Surrounding nothing no more! Imagine the walls
collapsing and the box disappearing into nothing and
that's what it becomes is nothing! It has really always been
nothing! We just ignorantly allowed it to exist! Imagine
nothing! Imagine something! Imagine anything! Imagine
everything! Imagine going far beyond the limits of gravity
and who could possibly stop you?! Imagine your world and
there it is! Imagine who you want to become and don't

worry about when it will transpire for you are already that flawless immaculate person! Imagine imagining! Imagine freedom and liberty… Imagine choosing who you are and decide to be that particular person! Fly out of the box with your imagination…

BEYOND THE MAYHEM

Snow must be warmer than me,
Nobody can thaw my forlornness,
I can't even buy a shadow,
I am frigidly alone,
Instead of pumping blood my immobile heart dilutes logic,
Now that my mask is inevitably slipping down beneath my
elusive face,
Emitting beams of deficiency that reveal this insecure
entropy,
Love's confidence is on the brink of narcissism,
Teetering on the inextirpable infatuation,
Merely existing,
I've lost everything except for my imagination,
Utter chaos unravels in my mind,
Remaining stoic is the ultimate shield,
Yet it is also the sharpest sword,
Forever I dwell in this fastidious misery,
Reach away from this bedlam…

FREEDOM'S CAGE

Azure sky invites us all in it,
Sun, moon, stars, clouds, and the fresh air that we breathe
are confined by it,
Mountains, beaches, forests, and deserts show the very
realm of it,
Water, sand, rocks, and the grass decorate the very
foundation of it,
We see it clear as crystal,
Yet cannot touch it,
Some bask in it,
While they assume it will be around forever,
It screams for unleashing,
It is the reason fire burns,
Its vulnerability detonates,
It drinks what we drown,
Soldiers fade into its vain war,
Opportunity of liberty thrives its ugly beauty,
Stubborn clock ticks its master,
Freedom's time locks its cage…

INTEGRITY'S SHADOW

Gravity suffocates her reflection,
I know because I looked deep into the realm of her
gorgeous eyes,
Still blind steel mind,
Run through her wet electricity,
Share all of this with her,
She can't though,
We could sigh,
We should fly,
We would buy,
Storms of fade churn in the shade,
Rusty emotions shine darker than any of mine,
Shifting tears crying gears,
Ladder of her illusion destroys this gamble,
Deploy the decoy of this ploy,
Prepare her for she doesn't know the cosmic truth,
Pithy magnanimous espionage manacles the swarthiest...

DERELICT FUEHRER IMMURES

Smoke until you convoke,
Drink until you chink,
Swallow until you hollow,
Snort until you mort,
Trip until you blip,
Cigarettes and beer,
Eddying behind the leer,
Weed and cocaine,
Atavistic rhapsody exemplify chicane,
Acid and psychedelic mushrooms,
Resurrected corpse exhumes,
Cheating the game is like a vampire bathing in blood
without being able to drink it because it's a capitulation…

SWALLOW THE LEADER

Perhaps you are wondering who established and built this ultimately invincible elite alliance,
Let your curiosity expire its me that you want and desire I am the one that burns the fire,
Ignite this plight that you excite with such extraordinary might,
We arrived to gander at the hungry sharks that decimated everything in the bloody ocean,
Neutralize gallant discipline,
Avarice juxtaposes quintessentially,
Reprievable galleys careen through this astern mirror of comeuppance,
Merge with the dregs of our platitudes,
Sobriety chokes our clarity,
Replete behest chagrined when your glyph verbally told us about the egalitarians,
Gabby silence doffs the circumventive cirrus,
Two sizzling hot banshees that wail with their kindred…

LINGUAL ENTITY MANACLED

Freedom of leech,
Restrain reality,
Sleeping aloof ebbed on the shore,
Dreaming about melting cold chains,
Burn through these ice shackles,
Frozen ghost haunts fire perihelion,
Run far away to the river of swimming scrutiny,
Ashen reservoir is responsible for this cosmic espionage,
Crescent migrates beneath her master's favorite bridge,
Slide up over her artifact's lame pond,
Disgusted by the repulsive image in the mirror,
Denying that it is yourself,
Bending the reflection until it breaks,
Shards of the jack in the fox mimic the Ace of Spades,
Umbrageous floe is not an argosy,
Caliginous billow rivets seismic aplomb,
Frigorific hero polishes its reverberant metaphor,
Participate in eminent domain's cozy mural,
Galvanic igloo suppresses this incredulous hearth,
Resuscitate this negligible prism's adoption,
She melted away with her jovial confetti,
Blood of hers never gulped my oddity's dirge…

SOLACE GLEG

Halloween night a wizard hatched from an egg,
Drank an entire keg,
Had sex with a women named Peg,
Until he broke his leg,
Afterwards she made him beg…

PARHELION INSECURITY

Desperately trying to be cool, eager to be accepted somewhere with somebody, wanting just a tiny piece of attention, hey anybody look at the pathetic me! Why does it matter so much?! They despise you without reason! Yet you still desire to be in the same place as them! Why?! They don't like you because your inferior personality sticks out so vulnerably into their pompous little world!

Yet you still force yourself to care about their insignificant existence! Forget them! If you possess some sort of contribution that benefits them or their policy then and only then will they flatter and coax you with feigned and fabricated empathy! Why?! Why I say?! Why continue to entertain this audacity?! Live in an artificial reality or die in a lonely isolation?! Talk to yourself and others will assume you crazy or waste time talking to them who listens not?! Do you hear yourself?! Is it me or you that I'm talking to?! Both?! Assumptions are atrocious even in despair…

Flooding your mind with sabotaged dreams of machicolation… Dived into the mirror with twisting and churning intentions… Identity crisis hangs in the balance of truth… Growing a discovery takes courage that won't wither away when fear arrives so spontaneously! Illegitimately questioning my effective methods when I have proven undoubtedly that I know exactly what I'm doing! Introspective disapproval gazes back at me, you, us, everyone recoiling from the mirror of reconciliation…

IRONY OF EPIGRAM

Honey frowns at the bees of summer,
Money smiles at the people of greed,
Intelligence laughs at the stupidity of tests,
Marriage vows at the bride of the groom,
Indeed jumps at the doubt of certainty,
Bleed injuries at the hospital of pain,
Water flows at the creek of dryness,
Beverages drink at the thirst of cups,
Blind sees at the vision of eyes,
Find searches at the lost of possession,
Theory intuits at the premonition of luck,
Heat freezes at the fire of cold,
Age births at the elders of youth,
Rage calms at the emotions of this nonsense poem!
What am I writing about?!
If you don't know then I am finished!

PLENTY OF BONES DOCTOR OSSUARY

Distant urn in sight,
Familiar feeling instigates,
Sky indulges in thunder and lightning,
Hurry the storm escalates,
Shall the clouds unravel and the rain collapse,
Pursue this peculiar idea of curiosity,
Penalize skeletons of battle,
Death lingers with the stench of corpses,
Warning poised trying to prevent this discovery,
Lazy snakes and scorpions invite any living organisms,
Bloody scent entices the humans,
Cactus smiles a slight danger,
Busy insects and reptiles glance in the wrong direction,
Chewing on their crematory stethoscopes with this silly asininity
that I am writing makes me wonder why I bother to write?!
Emphasize that poetry has no tenor...

SEPTIC STAINS INTACT

Love is a bombastic disease$
Hate is a philosophical remedy$
Confusion is a telepathic comrade$
Insanity is a contagious alimentation$
Life is a gauche pons asinorum$
Death is a chivalrous moxie$

NOTE OF APPRECIATION

Thanks to every single individual that I have come into contact with.
Whether positive or negative I have learned something from everybody.
Family, friends, acquaintances, strangers, enemies, etc.

THE DISTORTED SOUL,
RICHARD LAYTON FOLEY

Printed in the United States
By Bookmasters